Amazing Animal Facts

WRITTEN BY
CHRISTOPHER MAYNARD

DORLING KINDERSLEY • LONDON • NEW YORK • STUTTGART

A DORLING KINDERSLEY BOOK

Editor Deborah Murrell
Art Editor Hans Verkroost
Assistant Editor Claire Bampton
Assistant Designer Susan St. Louis
Managing Editor Sophie Mitchell
Managing Art Editor Miranda Kennedy
Production Paola Fagherazzi

Additional editorial assistance
Michèle Lynch and Jane Parker

First published in Great Britain in 1993 by
Dorling Kindersley Limited
9 Henrietta Street, London WC2E 8PS

Copyright text ©1993 Dorling Kindersley Limited, London
Copyright photography ©1993 Jerry Young and Dorling Kindersley
Copyright illustrations © 1993 Dorling Kindersley
Reprinted 1994, 1995

A CIP catalogue for this book is available from the British Library.
ISBN 0 7513 5069 9

Colour reproduction by Colourscan, Singapore
Printed and bound in Italy by Graphicom, Vicenza

Contents

What do bears eat?

BEARS EAT ALMOST ANYTHING, including fruit, nuts, leaves, and insects. Picnic leftovers, such as fish and meat, will also do nicely, and a snack of honey is something no bear can resist.

Do bears grizzle?

The grizzly didn't get its name because of its bad temper. In fact, the name comes from the white tips on the bear's fur. This makes it look "grizzled", or speckled with grey.

When do cubs scout?

These black bear cubs are four months old. They have already begun to scout around outside the den, but they still rely on their mother to find food. They will leave home when they are about two years old.

Bears will fight fiercely to defend their homes.

Brown bears, like this grizzly (right), have long hunting claws on their front paws.

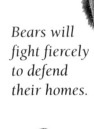

Do bears wear specs?

The spectacled bear looks as though it does. It got its name because of the dark fur around its eyes. Spectacled bears feed on fruit, and they often sleep in the trees after eating.

How heavy are bears?

The heaviest brown bear is the Kodiak bear, from Alaska. A large male can weigh more than 600 kg (1,323 lb). But polar bears, which live in the Arctic, are even bigger. An adult male can weigh 720 kg (1,587 lb).

What bugs bugs?

The little sun bear from Southeast Asia does - it keeps eating them! When it finds a big mound of delicious termites, it tears open the mound with its long claws and lets the termites swarm all over its paws. Then it slurps them up, dozens at a time, with its long tongue.

BEAR FACTS

- Black bears can gallop at up to 50 km/h (31 mph) in an emergency. They can also climb up trees to get out of danger.

- Bears are usually shy, but in the USA some black bears raid rubbish dumps for the delicious titbits people throw away.

- Polar bears can grow up to 2.5 m (8 ft) from their head to their tail.

- Teddy bears are named after Teddy Roosevelt, an American president who became very popular after he refused to shoot a bear cub in 1902.

When is it good to have a blocked nose?

When you're a sloth bear. This animal pokes its long snout into termite nests to suck up the insects. Fortunately, a sloth bear can close its nostrils to stop itchy termites from crawling up its nose.

DID YOU KNOW?
Pandas feed on bamboo, a tall, tough grass with very little goodness in it. An adult panda has to eat about 20 kg (44 lb) of bamboo stems a day.

Asian black bears are often called moon bears because of the white crescent on their chests.

Can bears dance?

All bears can stand and walk on their hind legs, and Asian black bears like this one can balance on two feet almost as well as you can. Sadly, this has tempted some people to catch black bear cubs and train them to dance in circuses and travelling fairs.

How do bears talk?

Bears use body language to communicate, as well as growls and grunts. A direct stare is a warning, and a bear with its head lowered is about to attack.

What keeps a polar bear warm?

Polar bears have a thick layer of fat under their skin, to keep heat in as they hunt for food in the icy Arctic Ocean. A polar bear can get so hot lying in the sun that it will jump into the sea just to cool down.

DID YOU KNOW?
Male bears scratch marks on trees to warn off other bears. The higher the mark, the bigger the bear.

Are dogs wild ?

MOST PET DOGS would not survive without us to feed them. But all dogs are related to wolves. Wolves probably once hunted with people, and then moved into their homes, gradually changing into the pets we have today. There are still more than thirty kinds of wild dogs, including coyotes, jackals, and dingos.

What do wild puppies eat?

Adult wild dogs hunt to provide food for their puppies. Often they chew the meat first to make it easier for the pups to eat with their tiny teeth.

Can dogs fight wars?

The ancestors of the Bernese mountain dog (below) pulled carts for Roman soldiers. And 4,000 years ago, people in the Middle East kept them for hunting and fighting.

The Bernese is one of four kinds of Swiss mountain dog.

Are toy dogs real?

Yes, they are. They get their name because of their size. The Pekingese was once a sacred pet of the Emperor of China. People had to bow to it, and the punishment for stealing a Pekingese was death.

Why do dogs live in packs?

Most wild dogs hunt, rest, and travel in groups called packs. This way of life makes good sense. The adults can protect the young pups, and by hunting as a pack, dogs can kill animals larger than they could ever manage on their own.

What is a hyena?

A hyena may look like a dog, but it is more closely related to weasels and cats. Hyenas probably look like dogs because they live in similar places, and hunt the same kinds of prey.

German shepherd dogs are sometimes called Alsatians.

Which dog is most like a wolf?

People have bred German shepherd dogs to look as much like wolves as possible. But their behaviour is no more wolf-like than any other dog's.

Can dogs do tricks?

Some dogs can. The Bichon Frisé was once very popular in French courts. But after the French Revolution, when the king and nobility were overthrown, many of these dogs were taken into circuses, and trained to perform tricks.

Do bush dogs live in bushes?

No, but they do live among them. A short tail and a small, thick body make it easy for this dog to move about in the undergrowth, as well as in its underground home.

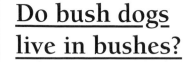

How many dogs make a pack?

African wild dogs working in packs of ten or twenty can hunt animals as large as antelopes or wildebeest. The leader grabs the prey to slow it down, then the rest mob it and drag it to the ground.

What are fire house dogs?

Dalmatians were once popular fire-station mascots, or "fire house dogs". Until cars became common at the beginning of this century, dalmatians also served as coach dogs, trotting by the wheels of carriages.

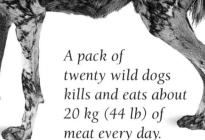

A pack of twenty wild dogs kills and eats about 20 kg (44 lb) of meat every day.

DOG FACTS

- Dogs have much better hearing than human beings. Wild dogs can hear a ticking watch from 10 m (30 ft) away.

- A coyote howls to warn other coyotes to stay out of its territory. It often finds a high place to howl from, so the sound can be heard over a larger area.

- Dogs can't retract (pull in) their claws as cats can, so you can always see the shape of the claws in their paw prints.

- A dog can build up a mental picture of another dog using only its sense of smell.

Do all dogs hunt?

All wild dogs hunt, but most pet dogs would starve if they were left to fend for themselves. Some breeds though, like this tough bull terrier, still have a powerful instinct for hunting.

What does a fox eat?

YOUR LEFTOVERS, PROBABLY. Foxes often make their way across fields or along overgrown railway tracks at night, to feed on the food that people throw into their rubbish bins.

Can foxes climb?

Most foxes are happiest on the ground. But the grey fox has an unusual ability – it can climb up and down the trunks of trees. It grips the bark with its front paws and pushes itself up with its back legs.

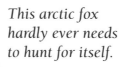

This arctic fox hardly ever needs to hunt for itself.

Where do Arctic foxes find food?

Arctic foxes are happy to eat a polar bear's leftovers. A fox will sometimes trail along after a bear, living very well on its scraps.

Grey foxes are also called tree foxes.

What can a fox hear?

This bat-eared fox's large ears pick up sounds that we could never hear. The fox needs good hearing to find the insects that it feeds on.

When do foxes pounce?

When they get close to a small animal, such as a mouse, foxes often leap into the air and pounce on it with both front paws, pinning the animal to the ground.

How small are fox cubs?

Fox cubs are tiny at birth. They weigh about 100 g (3.5 oz) and are no bigger than a mouse. They are blind, and totally dependent on their mother.

There are four kinds of desert foxes. They hide in the shadows of rocks for much of the day. All four kinds have large ears, which lose heat easily and help them to stay cool.

When do foxes change their coats?

Arctic foxes have a white winter coat that helps them hide in the snow. In spring the white fur falls out and the fox grows a brown summer coat.

How small are foxes?

The fennec fox (above) is one of the smallest foxes, with a body about 40 cm (16 in) long. It lives in the Sahara Desert, and feeds on insects.

The Arctic fox has a dark brown coat in summer.

Kit foxes sometimes signal with their tails to warn their young of danger.

Are foxes rare?

Kit foxes are. Once they were quite common, but because people have destroyed most of their habitat, only about 7,000 are left today.

When does a fox use a brush?

A brush is the name for a fox's tail. It is long, thick, and bushy, so it makes a cosy blanket in cold weather. The fox wraps its tail around its paws and face to keep warm.

FOX FACTS

- Foxes eat small animals, such as frogs, birds, and insects. But when prey is hard to find they also eat berries and fruits.

- A female fox is called a vixen, and her underground home is called an earth.

- The pads on a desert fox's paws are covered in fur, which protects them when they walk on hot rock and sand.

13

Is a wolf a dog?

WOLVES ARE THE LARGEST members of the dog family. They stand up to 1 m (3 ft) tall at the shoulder and can weigh as much as 50 kg (110 lb). When there is enough food, wolves live in packs, or groups, of up to twenty members.

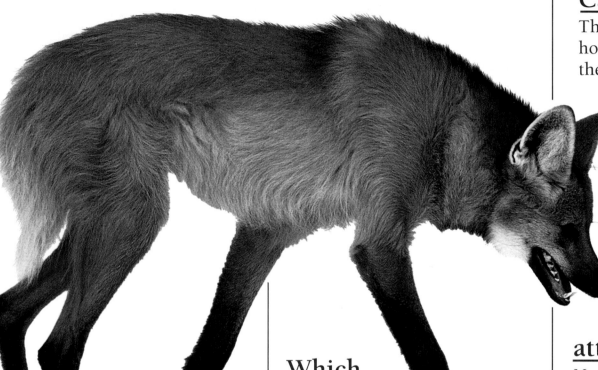

Can wolves sing?

They can't sing, but they can howl loudly! All the wolves in the pack, including the cubs, join in to warn other wolves to stay away from their territory.

Do wolves attack people?

Not unless they think they may be dangerous to them or their young. Most stories of wolves attacking people are untrue.

Which wolf isn't a wolf at all?

The maned wolf has long legs, just like a wolf. But it has bigger ears and a lighter body than a real wolf. This wild dog lives only in South America.

Why do wolves make trails?

Wolves leave trails of scent on trees, bushes, and rocks to warn off other wolves. A strange wolf entering another pack's territory will be chased away, or sometimes even killed.

Do wolves speak?

No, but they communicate very well with their face and body as well as their voice. Animals in a pack must know who the leader is, and obey his commands, for the pack to work well.

Do Arctic wolves eat Arctic hares?

The Arctic wolf usually feeds on caribou, or reindeer, but when food is scarce it will take whatever it can get. An Arctic hare makes a perfectly good meal for a hungry wolf.

This Arctic wolf is a kind of grey wolf. Its coat goes almost white in winter.

A wolf's strong legs are good for running long distances.

What colour is a grey wolf?

Despite its name, the grey wolf's coat is not always grey. It can be black, cream, brown, or a mixture of colours. Often, the coat is similar in colour to the wolf's surroundings, for camouflage (disguise).

How fast are wolves?

Wolves run fast only in short bursts. What they are best at is slow running, called loping. A pack often trails its prey in this way for hours, until the animal is so tired it can't run any more.

How many kinds of wolf are there?

Many kinds of dogs are called wolves, including the prairie wolf, or coyote, and the red wolf. But the grey wolf, also called the timber wolf, is the only true kind.

Do cubs hunt?

This wolf cub is much too small to hunt with the rest of the pack. It will not go scouting for food with the adults until it is about six months old.

WOLF FACTS

- Wolf cubs live on their mother's milk for the first few weeks of their lives, just like human babies.

- Wolves can reach speeds of up to 65 km/h (40 mph) in short bursts. They can also keep up a steady pace for many hours, covering vast distances.

- When a mother goes hunting, the father or another adult babysits the cubs until she returns with food.

Are big cats big?

COMPARED WITH PET CATS, they are giants! Strictly speaking, only five species of cats are called big cats. They are the lions, tigers, jaguars, leopards, and snow leopards. But there are many large wild cats besides these.

The leopard is good at climbing trees. Its long tail helps it to balance.

Do cats like water?

Some do. Tigers are strong swimmers and they often wade into water to cool off. They sometimes even catch frogs and fish to snack on.

How fast are cats?

The cheetah is the fastest land animal. It can run at about 90 km/h (56 mph), but only for a short way, and in a straight line. A fast antelope can often escape a cheetah.

Are spots useful?

Leopards are covered in spots. Although their markings help hide them against their background, they also cause the deaths of many leopards every year, because people want their beautiful skins for fur coats.

When do leopards hunt?

Leopards spend the day lazing about in the branches of trees. When evening comes, they climb down and set off alone to hunt. Sometimes they simply lie in wait on a branch and pounce on an antelope or other animal passing below the tree.

DID YOU KNOW?
The caracal is not a big cat, but it is not very small, either. It lives in the desert, and hunts in the cool of the night for hares, lizards, and other animals. It can jump so high and fast that it can catch birds as they fly past.

How do lions roar?

The voice box of a big cat, unlike other cats, is joined to its skull. This is what gives it its loud roar. When a big cat purrs, it has to pause for breath every so often. Small cats purr nonstop, but they can't roar.

Lions are the only cats that live in family groups, called prides.

What do lions eat?

Almost anything they can catch, including wildebeest, zebras, and buffaloes. Lionesses (female lions) do most of the work, hunting in teams. One lioness drives it towards the others, who bring it to the ground and kill it with a quick bite to the throat.

Can a leopard change its spots?

Not whenever it chooses, but there is a kind of leopard whose spots have faded so much that they are hardly visible. This animal is known as the black panther, and it is most common in parts of India.

How do cats hide?

By being still. Resting in a tree, a leopard is almost invisible among the shadows. But a flick of the tail can give it away.

Do pumas have spots?

Pumas are born with spotted coats, but after about three months they begin to fade. At about six months old pumas are red-brown all over.

Puma, mountain lion, and cougar are all different names for the same cat.

BIG CAT FACTS

- In India, legend says leopards are so cunning that they brush away their tracks with their tails.

- The snow leopard has a white coat with dark spots. It is easy to mistake one for a snow-speckled rock if it sits very still.

- Tigers are the biggest cats of all. A large Siberian tiger can weigh over 200 kg (441 lb).

17

Do all cats hunt?

THEY CERTAINLY DO. Cats are great climbers, runners, and jumpers, and this makes them good hunters. They have many more bones in their body than you do, and they can stretch and bend in ways that you can only dream about. They also have sharp claws for attacking and gripping prey.

Why is it hard to spot some cats?

The leopard cat is a small wild cat. Its spotted coat makes it look like a small leopard, and works in the same way to camouflage it from its prey.

Why do cats play with their food?

Sometimes a cat catches a mouse or a bird and plays with it instead of eating it. This helps improve the cat's killing skills. It takes a long time for a kitten to learn how to hunt, and even adult cats have to stay in practice.

Do pets paddle?

Most cats hate water, although they can all swim. But the Turkish swimming cat loves to paddle in shallow pools and streams. It has no thick underfur, so it dries off quickly.

Why do cats lick their paws?

To clean their fur. Cats have very rough tongues that remove all the dirt and brush their fur smooth. But a cat's tongue won't reach around its ears, so it has to lick its paws first, and use them to wash with instead.

What is a tail for?

A tail helps a cat balance. As the cat launches itself into the air it flicks its tail straight up, then holds it stiffly until it lands safely on the ground.

Cats push off with their long back legs, stretch out full length, and land on their short, strong front legs.

18

Do cats have nine lives?

Of course not – this saying began because cats are so good at surviving a fall. They twist their bodies in midair to land safely on their feet.

SMALL CAT FACTS

- When an Abyssinian cat miaows, it sounds like a bird singing.

- The smallest wild cat is the rusty-spotted cat of India. It usually weighs less than 1.5 kg (3 lb).

- A cat's eyes glow in the dark because a special layer at the back reflects light like a mirror.

DID YOU KNOW?
Cats eat grass to help them cough up fur they swallowed during grooming.

Are black cats lucky?

In some parts of America and Europe a black cat crossing your path is said to bring bad luck. In other countries, a black cat is a sign of good luck.

Why do cats arch their backs?

Pet cats purr when they are happy, and hiss when they are angry. A frightened cat arches its back and makes its fur stand on end to make itself look bigger to its enemy.

What is a bobcat?

A bobcat is a medium-sized North American wild cat. It has a short, stubby bobtail, tufted ears, and a ruff of fur behind the head. Bobcats hunt at night, feeding on rabbits and birds.

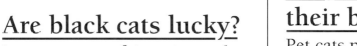

Are bats birds?

BATS HAVE WINGS and can fly well, so they look a bit like birds. But they are really mammals. There are more than 1,000 kinds of bats. They live in tropical rainforests, woods, caves, and towns.

Bats often roost together in a cave during the day.

Why do bats sleep upside down?

Because it's comfortable. Bats have to sleep this way because their legs are not strong enough to stand, and they cannot grip with their hands. The only way they can relax enough to sleep is by hanging upside down, holding on with their feet.

Do bats drink blood?

Only vampire bats have a taste for blood. They live in Central and South America, and at night they feed on the blood of sleeping horses and cattle. Most other kinds of bats live on insects, or fruit and nectar. A few even eat fish.

Do bats have hands?

Bats' hands have changed into wings, with a sheet of thin skin stretched between very long finger bones.

DID YOU KNOW? In summer, bats often get too hot. So they find a cool, dark place to rest in, such as a cupboard or a wardrobe. You could find a bat inside your clothes!

How blind is a bat?

People often use the phrase "as blind as a bat". In fact, bats are not blind at all. They can see perfectly well in daylight. But at night, their eyesight is just like yours – not very good!

Bats use their tails for balance.

Do bats take their babies to nurseries?

Although female bats only have two or three babies a year, they all have them at the same time. So they take care of them in large groups, called nurseries. Some nurseries can contain up to a million babies.

DID YOU KNOW? Female bats with no young of their own often join a nursery and help the other females care for their young.

Do bats make tents?

There is a bat in Central America that makes tents. This tiny fruit-eating bat bites along the strong rib in the middle of a palm leaf so that the sides fold down over it like a tent.

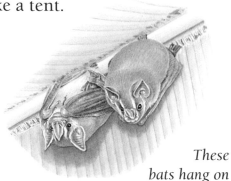

These bats hang on to the leaf by tucking their feet through the holes they have made.

When does a bat have a ball?

When it finds a cloud of insects in the dark. Many bats can't see at night, when they hunt. These bats use a trick called echolocation to find food – and to stop them bumping into things! As the bat flies along, it makes high-pitched squeaks. When these hit an insect, they bounce back. The bat hears the echo, and finds the insect.

What do bats do in winter?

Some bats live in places where there is no food for them in winter. They choose a quiet shelter, such as a hollow tree or a cave, where they fall into a deep sleep, called hibernation. A hibernating bat breathes so slowly that it is hard to tell whether it is alive or dead.

Hibernating close together helps stop bats losing too much moisture.

A bat's wings need to be kept in good condition for flying.

Long, strong toes can grip branches.

When is a bat a fox?

When it's a flying fox. Some fruit bats are called flying foxes because of their ginger-coloured fur, large brown eyes, and pointed noses.

DID YOU KNOW? This bulldog bat goes fishing using the special hooks on its back legs.

BAT FACTS

- Young bats can usually fly by the time they are four months old.

- The largest bats are flying foxes. Some flying foxes have a wingspan of more than 1 m (3 ft).

- The bumblebee bat is the smallest, at about 3 cm (1 in) long – the size of your big toe.

- The only bat that can walk along the ground is the vampire bat.

Are apes like us?

APES AND MONKEYS ARE more closely related to humans than any other animal. You can see this in their faces and hands. You may also see them chatter and play games, and there's nothing more human than that!

Where do lemurs live?

Lemurs are small primates that live only on the island of Madagascar, in the Indian Ocean. This aye-aye is a small, bushy-tailed kind of lemur. The aye-aye is almost extinct.

What is a primate?

Primates are mammals that have adapted to living in trees and, in some cases, on the ground as well. Apes, lemurs, and gorillas are all primates. But the most common primates are human beings.

When do baboons mate?

The red, swollen area under the tail of this female hamadryas baboon is a clear sign that she is at her most fertile. If she mates now, there is a good chance that she will produce young.

The De Brazza's monkey's long tail helps it to balance in forest trees.

How good is a gibbon's balance?

Very good indeed – even a female with her young can travel quickly through the forest, running along branches like a tightrope walker.

MONKEY FACTS

- Just like people, monkeys live in families. A really big troop might contain as many as fifty monkeys.

- Gibbons and humans are the only primates that can walk comfortably on their hind legs.

- The biggest primate of all is the gorilla. It weighs 3,000 times as much as the grey mouse lemur, which is the smallest primate.

Which animal is named after us?

The orang-utan (left) looks so much like us that people made its name up out of the Malay words for 'man' and 'forest'.

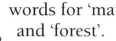

What makes a monkey attractive?

In the case of the proboscis monkey, it is the large nose, or proboscis, that gives it its name. In the breeding season the male with the largest nose is the one most females choose to mate with.

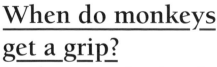

This owl monkey can see so well in the dark that it can catch insects as they fly past.

What do monkeys do at night?

Most monkeys curl up and go to sleep at night. But the owl monkey goes hunting. It gets its name from its owl-like hoot and huge eyes.

When do monkeys get a grip?

Monkeys can grip when they are born. It is often up to the baby to hold on to an adult as tightly as it can, like this golden lion tamarin clinging to his mother's fur.

Tails that grasp like this are called prehensile tails.

Do monkeys have five arms?

No, but many monkeys, like this spider monkey, can use their tail like an extra arm. This way they can hang from a branch and still have their hands free for eating.

Can monkeys learn new tricks?

All monkeys are fast learners, but macaques are especially clever. They pick up tricks from each other very quickly indeed. A crab-eating macaque (above) learns from its parents how to fish for crabs, and how to get the meat out of the shell.

Chimps make and use tools, just as we do.

Are chimps smart?

Chimpanzees are among the cleverest animals in the world. They even make tools by ripping the leaves off thin sticks and poking them into anthills to draw out ants.

What are mammals?

MAMMALS ARE WARM-BLOODED ANIMALS. They give birth to live young, which feed on their mother's milk. Elephants, whales, and porcupines are all mammals, as well as humans and apes.

Why do gorillas beat their own chests?

To settle an argument. Two males will roar, bark, tear up leaves, and beat their own chests. Usually the smaller gorilla backs down without a fight taking place.

How do walruses keep from freezing?

The walrus has a layer of thick fat, called blubber, under its skin to help it keep out the cold of its Arctic home.

A blue whale can hear another's song from up to 850 km (528 miles) away.

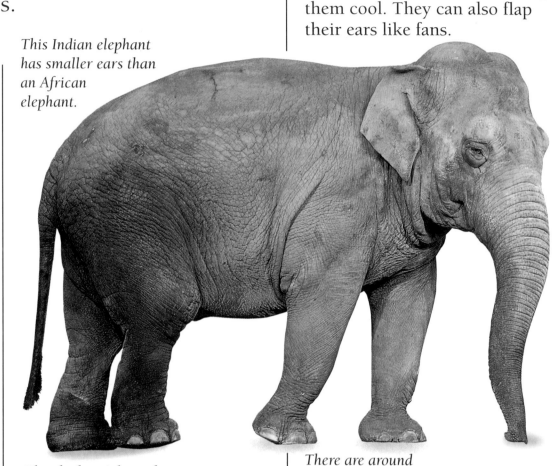

This Indian elephant has smaller ears than an African elephant.

The elephant's huge feet stop it sinking into soft ground.

Are mammals large?

Some are. The elephant is the largest land animal, but the ocean-dwelling blue whale is many times bigger. A female can grow to be 33 m (108 ft) long. Blue whales eat about 4 tonnes a day of tiny, shrimp-like creatures, called krill.

How do elephants keep cool?

By using their ears. Elephants live in the hottest parts of Africa and India, but their huge ears lose a lot of body heat and keep them cool. They can also flap their ears like fans.

There are around 60,000 muscles in an elephant's trunk.

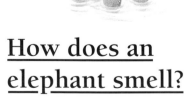

How does an elephant smell?

With its trunk. But an elephant's trunk is not just for smelling. It also uses it to pull food into its mouth, to suck up and squirt water for washing and drinking, and to call to other elephants.

Does a camel have one hump or two?

Dromedaries, or Arabian camels, have one hump. But bactrian camels, like this one, have two.

Are rhinoceroses thick-skinned?

Very. Their skin protects them from other animals. Insects cannot bite or sting through a rhino's skin, and even the sharp claws of a big cat cannot tear it.

Why do musk oxen make circles?

To protect their young. If wolves come near, the adults form a circle around the young. No matter where a wolf attacks, it always faces a set of horns.

DID YOU KNOW?
The hippopotamus gets its name from the Ancient Greek words for "river" and "horse".

Why do mammals drink milk?

Mammals are too weak to feed themselves when they are born, so their mothers provide them with milk. A mother's milk is full of goodness, and it contains everything a baby needs.

Rhinos are famous for their bad tempers. The only animal that dares attack them is a human with a gun.

MAMMAL FACTS

- The bumblebee bat is the smallest mammal in the world. It is less than 1/1000 the length of a blue whale.

- The only egg-laying mammals alive today are the platypus and the echidna. All other mammals give birth to live young.

- Human babies develop inside their mother for nine months. Elephant babies develop for 22 months, longer than any other mammal.

When do pandas climb trees?

When they are tired. Pandas sleep a lot to save energy. Often they climb a tree and wedge themselves into a comfortable notch in the branches. Here they are safe from enemies, and from falling out of the tree!

What are shells for?

AN ANIMAL'S SHELL usually protects the soft parts of its body. The largest group of animals with shells is the mollusc group, which includes snails, clams, mussels, and whelks.

How do snails make shells?

Pond snails live in water that has lots of chalk in it. They use this to build their shells. As their bodies grow they add to the open end of the shell to make it bigger.

Giant clams get much of their food from tiny, simple plants, called algae.

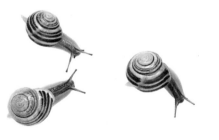

How big can a mollusc grow?

The giant clam (right) is the biggest mollusc in the world. It can weigh more than two adult humans. The part of the clam's skin that builds the shell is called the mantle.

Do snails form bands?

The European striped snail makes a shell with regular bands all around it. The bands are usually similar in colour to the snail's habitat, and help it to blend in with its surroundings.

What if you get too big for your shell?

When this nautilus grows too big for its shell it moves, but it doesn't leave home. It just builds a bigger chamber, seals off the old one, and moves into the new one. The old chambers fill with air, and help the nautilus to float.

Why do scallops clap?

Because that's how they swim. When a scallop is alarmed it quickly claps the two halves of its shell together. Water shoots out in one direction, and the scallop scoots off in another.

Are shells dangerous?

Cone shells are among the most beautiful shells in the world. And the animals inside them are deadly. They shoot a poison dart into their prey to paralyze it. The poison of one kind of cone shell is strong enough to kill a person.

This apple snail has been especially bred by people for its beautiful yellow shell.

Can whelks walk?

Whelks are small, marine (sea-living) snails that live just below the tide line. They have a single, large foot containing muscles that move in waves to push the animal slowly along.

What lays its eggs in a cloud?

Once a year, giant clams release a cloud of billions of eggs into the water. Most of the eggs will not be fertilized, and of those that are, most will be eaten.

Do snails have hands?

No, but they are often called left-handed or right-handed. Most snail shells coil in a clockwise direction. These are right-handed shells. But those that coil anti-clockwise are left-handed.

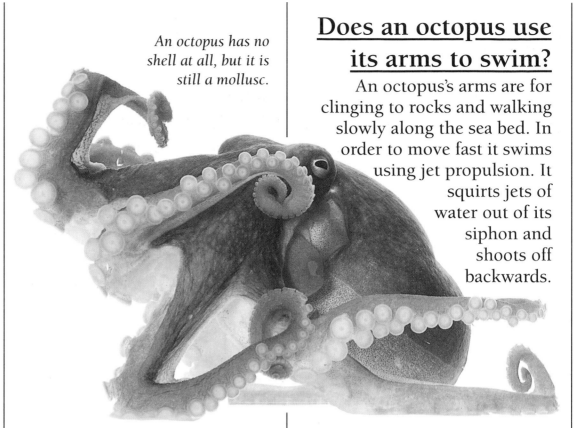

An octopus has no shell at all, but it is still a mollusc.

Does an octopus use its arms to swim?

An octopus's arms are for clinging to rocks and walking slowly along the sea bed. In order to move fast it swims using jet propulsion. It squirts jets of water out of its siphon and shoots off backwards.

Are slugs plants?

Many sea slugs look like bright, frilly plants. In fact, they are related to snails, although they don't have outer shells. They are protected by their nasty taste, and their bright colours warn enemies that they are not good to eat.

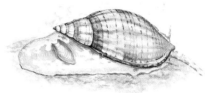

Can a snail shut its shell?

Many snails have a tough disc, called an operculum, on their foot. The snail can pull the operculum up to block the opening of its shell, and protect its soft body.

MOLLUSC FACTS

- An octopus can change colour to match its background in seconds, so it can hide almost anywhere.

- Most water snails have heavier shells than land snails. But they can still move because the water supports some of the weight.

- The giant land snail lays eggs about 2.5 cm (1 in) wide. People sometimes mistake them for birds' eggs.

Who needs knees?

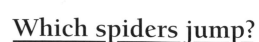

YOU DO, AND SO DO SPIDERS. They all have eight legs, and each leg has six joints. That's like having 48 knees. With all those joints it's not surprising that spiders can wave their legs in almost any direction.

The Chilean red-leg spider is so big it sometimes feeds on mice and birds.

Do spiders shut doors?

Trap-door spiders shut themselves in burrows to protect themselves from their enemies. This one plugs the entrance with its flat, hard abdomen (rear end). Others use mud, or weave doors out of silk.

Which spider has the hairiest legs?

The Chilean red-leg is one of the hairiest spiders in the world. It has eight eyes, but none of them can see well. So it uses the long hairs on its legs as feelers to find its way around.

How do young scorpions travel?

A female scorpion carries her babies around on her back until they are about two weeks old. If one falls off, she stops and waits while it climbs back up. Female scorpions defend their young with their claws and their stings.

A scorpion's claw is a useful weapon.

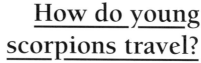

Which spiders jump?

Jumping spiders like this one pounce on their prey the way cats pounce on mice. They often spin a safety rope of silk thread, which they anchor to the ground before they leap.

DID YOU KNOW? Scorpions and spiders both belong to the group of animals called arachnids.

Although they are related, these two animals sometimes fight over food.

Do spiders have hairy escapes?

Bird-eating spiders, such as the one above, do. They use their back legs to flick the prickly hairs on their abdomen at an attacker. Each hair is shaped like a harpoon, and makes the enemy itch and sneeze.

How do spiders bite?

With their fangs. Most spiders' fangs work like pincers. But some big spiders have fangs that point downwards, which they stab into prey.

Do spiders eat each other?

When the tiny male black widow spider approaches a female for mating, he is in great danger of being eaten. So he gives her a big fresh insect wrapped in silk to eat instead.

Do spiders get caught in their own webs?

Garden spiders weave sticky webs to catch their prey. But the spider's feet are coated with oil, so it doesn't get trapped itself.

Some female crab spiders can change their colour to match a particular flower.

Changing colour can take up to three days.

Do spiders like flowers?

Crab spiders are fond of flowers the same colour as they are. They sit very still on the petals, so flying insects can't see them. As soon as an insect lands on the flower, the spider pounces.

Can spiders kill people?

This Brazilian wandering spider is poisonous enough to kill a person. A bite from a black widow or a funnel-web spider can also be deadly if an antidote is not given in time.

Can spiders swim?

Many spiders live near water, but only the water spider lives in it. Like all spiders, it has to breathe air, so it spins a bell-shaped web below the surface and fills it with bubbles of air.

SPIDER FACTS

- A spider's thread is stronger than the same thickness of steel.

- The black orb weaver uses enough silk in its web to wrap 40 times around this book.

- Some tiny spiders can travel for many kilometres on the wind. They spin a tangle of silk threads, which works rather like a parachute.

- Sprays that kill most spiders just make funnel-web spiders even more angry and dangerous.

Are beetles rare?

THERE ARE AT LEAST 350,000 different kinds of beetles. They are the most common insects. And they live just about everywhere in the world, except in places covered in ice and snow.

Which beetles have huge snouts?

Weevils are sometimes called snout beetles. This is because many have amazingly long snouts. Female weevils use their snouts to drill holes in plants, where they lay their eggs.

Who likes ladybirds?

Gardeners are always happy to give a home to ladybirds. Most ladybirds have a really big appetite for greenfly and blackfly, two kinds of insects that cause damage to plants.

Which beetle does nobody love?

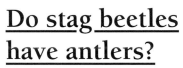

American farmers and gardeners hate the Colorado beetle because it eats potato plants. But before people introduced potatoes to the USA, these beetles fed only on wild desert plants.

DID YOU KNOW?
The larvae (young) of the arrow poison beetle are not born poisonous. But poison from the leaves they feed on stays in their body and protects them from enemies.

Do stag beetles have antlers?

Stag beetles got their name because their huge jaws look like a stag's antlers. The males use their jaws for wrestling in the breeding season, just as real stags do. Their jaws aren't as dangerous as they look, so the beetles don't usually get hurt.

Whirligigs look a bit like little rowing boats.

Can beetles swim?

Whirligigs are little beetles that skim over the surface of ponds and lakes like tiny, upturned boats, using their legs like oars. They often spin around in circles, which is what gave them their name. But nobody knows quite why they spin.

BEETLE FACTS

- Deathwatch beetles tap messages to each other from their tunnels inside old wooden beams and floorboards.

- Some beetles live on the fur of mice. They eat the larvae of the fleas that also live there.

Deathwatch beetles

- Carpet beetles eat not only carpets, but curtains, clothes, and even stuffed animals.

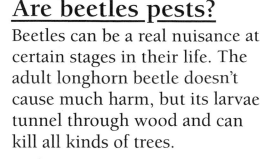

Do beetles play ball?

Dung beetles roll dung (animal droppings) into balls, just as we make snowballs. Then they roll the balls into their burrows. The females lay their eggs in the dung so their young have plenty of food when they hatch out.

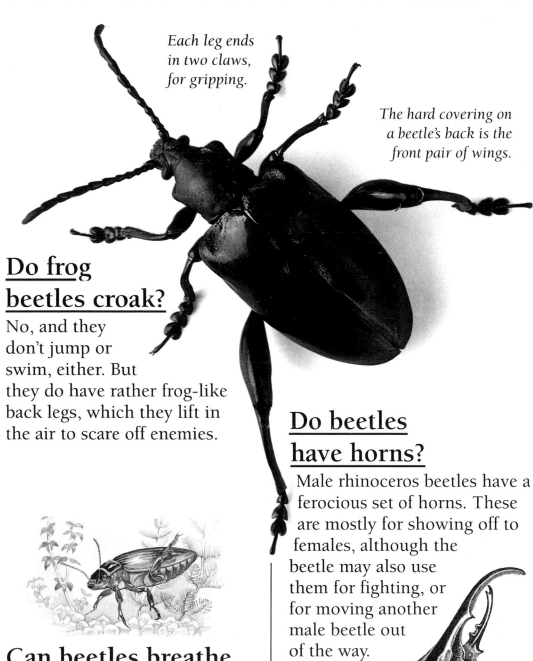

Each leg ends in two claws, for gripping.

The hard covering on a beetle's back is the front pair of wings.

Do frog beetles croak?

No, and they don't jump or swim, either. But they do have rather frog-like back legs, which they lift in the air to scare off enemies.

Do beetles have horns?

Male rhinoceros beetles have a ferocious set of horns. These are mostly for showing off to females, although the beetle may also use them for fighting, or for moving another male beetle out of the way.

Can beetles breathe under water?

The great diving beetle can. It stores bubbles of air under its front wings, and breathes this air while it is under water.

Are beetles pests?

Beetles can be a real nuisance at certain stages in their life. The adult longhorn beetle doesn't cause much harm, but its larvae tunnel through wood and can kill all kinds of trees.

Why do bees sting?

BEES STING TO DEFEND THEMSELVES or their hive. A honeybee's sting is barbed like a fish hook, and usually stays in the flesh of the animal it has stung. When this happens the bee dies, so it doesn't use its sting unless it really needs to.

A female potter wasp never sees her young. Once she has closed the nest she flies off.

Do wasps make pots?

Potter wasps do. Before a female lays an egg she builds a little mud pot. Into it she places the egg and a fresh caterpillar, which the young wasp, called a larva, will eat when it hatches.

What do hunting wasps hunt?

Anything that their young can eat, such as caterpillars, beetles, and spiders. But the adults do not usually eat meat themselves – they feed mostly on fruit juice and nectar from flowers.

Are wasps sociable?

Most kinds of wasp, like this tarantula-eating wasp, live alone. But some, including the common wasp, build papery nests, where they live and bring up their young in groups.

Do all bees live in hives?

We often think of bees as insects that live in large groups. In fact, most of the 19,000 different kinds of bees live on their own.

What makes bees swarm?

When a new queen is born, the hive splits in two. A great swarm of bees leaves with one queen to find a new home.

A swarm often rests on a tree while a few bees go out looking for a good nesting site.

How long do bees live?

A queen honeybee may live for as long as five years. A queen bumblebee dies once she has raised a colony of her own, which she often does in her first year. Worker bees are born in spring and die out in autumn.

A queen bumblebee's first batch of eggs always hatches into workers.

32

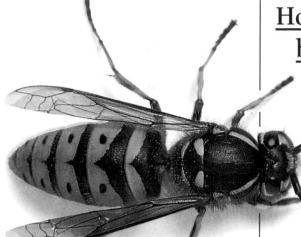

How different are bees from wasps?

Wasps feed their young on insects and spiders, but bees gather nectar and pollen from flowers to feed theirs. Bees have bodies covered in hair, but wasps usually have hairless bodies.

How is honey made?

When a bee visits a flower it sucks up the sweet nectar. It carries this back to the hive in a special honey stomach. Other bees mix it with a liquid from their mouths and pour the mixture into the honeycomb. After about three days the liquid turns into honey.

How do paperwasps make their nests?

Paperwasps build paper nests. They chew tree fibres into pulp, which they use to mould a nest. The pulp dries as a light, but very tough material.

Why do bees dance?

The pattern a bee makes in its dance describes how far away and in what direction food can be found. A circular dance means pollen and nectar can be found less than 50 m (165 ft) away. A figure-of-eight dance means the food is further away.

Do wasps dig holes?

The female jewel wasp digs a hole in the ground to make a nest for her egg. She moves grains of sand with her jaws and uses her legs to kick away loose bits and pieces.

BEE & WASP FACTS

- Cuckoo bees lay their eggs in the nests of other bees. This way they avoid all the hard work of running a hive.

- Honeybees visit shallow, open flowers to get nectar. Bumblebees have longer tongues, so they can go to flowers with deeper cups.

- Some tiny wasps, called chalcids, lay their eggs in the eggs of other insects. The chalcid wasp's young hatch out first, and feed on the host egg.

- The black and yellow wasps you see in the garden all make a kind of paper for their nests.

Are moths shy?

YOU DON'T SEE MOTHS as often as you see butterflies. This is not because they are shy, but because most of them fly at night, when you are asleep. There are many more kinds of moths than butterflies.

What's hairy and tastes bad?

Tiger moth caterpillars look like fat, hairy worms. They have such a nasty taste that most birds leave them alone. The only bird that eats these juicy morsels is the cuckoo.

How do moths hide?

Moths that fly at night have to be well disguised so that they can rest safely during the day. This oleander hawk moth has a pattern on its back and wings that makes it almost invisible on oleander leaves.

Can moths sting?

Moths have no stings, but some kinds fool enemies into thinking that they do. This European moth is harmless. But because it looks like a hornet, which stings, other animals don't attack it.

DID YOU KNOW? This winter moth lives only during the winter months. The female has no wings, but she doesn't need them. After emerging from her pupa, she only has to crawl up a tree to lay her eggs.

How well do moths smell?

Moths have an amazing sense of smell. Females attract males by giving off a special perfume. A male can smell it from several kilometres away with its big, feathery antennae. It follows the scent directly to the female.

Do moths use straws?

Like butterflies, many moths sip nectar. They push their long, straw-like tongue, called a proboscis, to the bottom of flowers. This hawk moth has a proboscis about three times the length of its body. When it is not feeding, the moth rolls its proboscis up like a spring.

This teleomoth's long, feathery antennae are good for picking up scents.

MOTH FACTS

- Most moths fly at night when the air is cold, so many of them have fat, hairy bodies to keep the warmth in.

- The Asian vampire moth can pierce the skin of an animal to drink its blood.

- Some moths have no mouths. Instead of eating, they survive on energy they stored up as caterpillars.

- We taste food with our tongues, but moths taste with their feet.

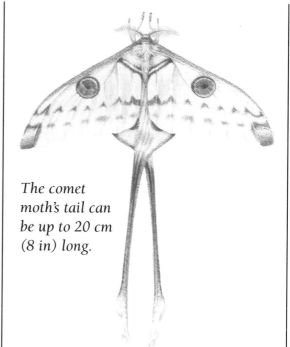

The comet moth's tail can be up to 20 cm (8 in) long.

Is it a bird?

The biggest moths in the world have wings the size of a bird's. This atlas moth, from Southeast Asia, is as big as a blackbird. It stretches 30 cm (12 in) from wing tip to wing tip. Even its caterpillars are about twice as long as your middle finger.

The atlas moth has a pattern on its wing tips that looks like a snake's head.

Do moths need tails?

Lots of moths have tails on their wings to disguise their shape. This comet moth has one of the longest tails of all. Its head is quite well hidden, so any bird that spots it will probably peck at the trailing tail, giving the moth a good chance of escape.

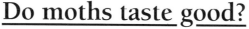

Do moths taste good?

The cinnabar moth's black and red wing colours warn birds that it tastes terrible. The moth's body is so tough that it is rarely hurt even if a bird pecks at it by mistake. But the bird gets a mouthful of bad-tasting liquid, and flies off in disgust.

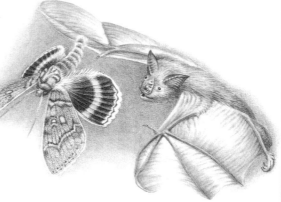

Can moths hear?

Some moths have an eardrum on each side of their body. They use the eardrums to listen out for the high-pitched squeaks of a bat as it homes in on them in the dark. This advance warning gives these moths a few extra seconds to get out of the bat's way.

How much lunch can a caterpillar munch?

From the moment they are born, caterpillars spend their time stuffing themselves. These little eating machines have only one aim – to grow big enough to turn themselves into moths.

What is a butterfly?

BUTTERFLIES ARE INSECTS, closely related to moths. They fly by day, unlike most moths, which fly at night. When they rest, butterflies fold their wings over their backs. Moths hold their wings out flat.

How many wings do butterflies have?

Butterflies have four wings, two in front and two at the back. The wings look delicate, but in fact they are very strong.

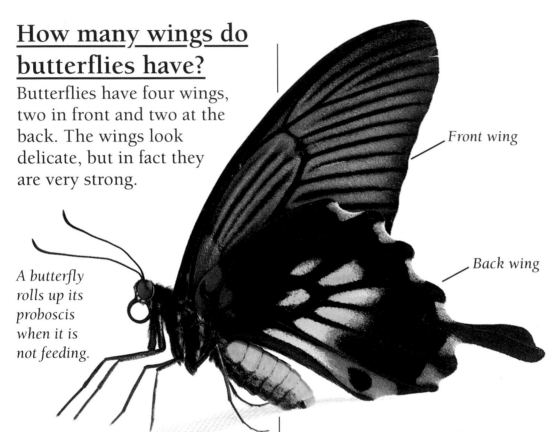

Front wing

Back wing

A butterfly rolls up its proboscis when it is not feeding.

How well can butterflies see?

Butterflies have two big, bulging compound eyes, made of hundreds of simple lenses. They see everything as a patchwork of tiny pictures.

Do butterflies fly far?

Every autumn, thousands of monarch butterflies migrate thousands of kilometres from North America to Mexico. They spend the winter there in the warmer weather.

What is a chrysalis?

A chrysalis is the halfway stage between a caterpillar and a butterfly. The caterpillar spins a silk cocoon to protect and disguise itself. While the caterpillar is in the cocoon, changing its shape, it is called a chrysalis. The butterfly that eventually climbs out of the cocoon has damp, crumpled wings. These must dry out before it can fly.

Which butterfly has eyes on its wings?

The owl butterfly has huge eyespots on its wings. When it is at rest with its wings closed, it could easily be mistaken for a real owl.

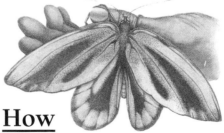

How big are butterflies?

Queen Alexandra birdwing butterflies are as big as starlings. The males are a beautiful, bright blue. Sadly, collectors have killed so many of these butterflies that they are now protected by law.

How many eyes do caterpillars have?

Most caterpillars have twelve eyes, but their eyesight is poor. They can only tell the difference between light and dark. Some caterpillars have no eyes at all. They get around by touch and smell alone.

How do butterflies hide themselves?

This comma butterfly hides from its enemies by staying still. It looks like a torn leaf on a twig, and the white "comma" in the middle of the back wing looks like a hole in the leaf.

Why do some butterflies like mud?

In hot countries, patches of damp earth attract large flocks of butterflies. They fly in to drink straight from the ground.

What do butterflies eat and drink?

Butterflies suck up the sweet nectar from flowers. They drink dew, or water from ponds or streams.

Where do butterflies sleep?

At night butterflies find a quiet place on a twig or leaf, or at the top of a blade of grass. Often they sleep in the same place night after night because they know it is safe.

DID YOU KNOW?
The tiger butterfly (above right) is poisonous, so birds don't touch it. Many other butterflies have the same colours and patterns, so they are safe from birds, too.

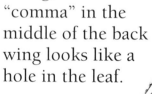

Butterflies have six legs, like most insects.

BUTTERFLY FACTS

- Two butterflies may battle over a favourite patch of sunshine. Luckily they cannot hurt each other.

- Some butterflies sip the juices of rotten fruit. The juices contain alcohol, and sometimes a butterfly gets so drunk it can't fly!

- People often say "I have butterflies in my tummy" when they are worried and can feel their stomach fluttering.

What are frogs?

FROGS ARE AMPHIBIANS, and so are toads, newts, and salamanders. Amphibians are animals that are born in water and spend the early part of their life there. Most only learn to move around on land as they get older.

Can a leaf croak?

You might think so, if you came across an Asian leaf frog. This little frog lives on the forest floor. Its brown skin, jagged shape, and hooded eyes make it look like a dead leaf.

What's for lunch?

This horned frog has an appetite to match the size of its mouth. It eats worms, insects, other frogs, rats - in fact, anything that it can fit in!

The horned frog has no teeth, so it swallows its meals whole.

Which frogs have foamy feet?

Some tree frogs produce a liquid that they tread into a stiff foam with their feet. They lay their eggs in this foam, and it dries to form a shell. This protects the eggs while they develop.

What are tadpoles?

Tadpoles are baby frogs, although they don't look much like them. They breathe through gills, like fish, and spend all their time swimming, and feeding on small plants and animals. After a time little legs sprout, the tail shrinks, and the tadpole soon becomes a small frog.

The mole and the mole frog both have wide, shovel-shaped front feet that are perfect for digging.

Which frog looks like a mole?

The mole frog of Australia has a small, mole-like head with a rounded snout and tiny eyes. It even digs head first, like a mole, and uses its strong front legs to sweep aside the sand as it hunts for insects.

Are frogs poisonous?

Some are. This tiny dart-poison frog has a bright blue and black pattern to warn other animals that its skin is poisonous.

This red-eyed tree frog can leap right out of the water to catch a meal.

Are frogs fast movers?

Frogs move fast when it comes to grabbing a meal. They may sit still for ages, waiting for an insect to come near. The moment it does, they leap at it like lightning and gulp it down.

This White's tree frog has sticky pads on its fingers and toes which help it cling to branches.

Are frogs friendly?

White's tree frog is quite happy to live on tree branches, but it often hops into people's homes, too. Once inside, it heads for cool, moist places, like sinks and bathtubs.

FROG FACTS

- The smallest frog is a cousin of the poison-dart frogs. It is only about 12 mm (half an inch) long.

- The glass frog has see-through skin. If you look closely you can see its heart beating.

- A dwarf puddle frog is about the size of your thumb. But it can eat 100 mosquitoes in a single night.

- Some horned frogs have a croak that sounds like a cow mooing.

Which frog has eyes on its back?

The false-eyed frog. If it is attacked from behind, it bends over to frighten the enemy off with its two huge eyespots.

Can frogs climb?

Some tree frogs are such good climbers that they spend their entire life up in the trees. These frogs eat, sleep, and lay their eggs among branches and leaves, so they never need to come down to the ground.

Do frogs eat eggs?

The Australian stomach-brooding frog swallows her eggs. They develop inside her stomach, and jump out of her mouth when they have grown into tiny frogs.

To keep their skin moist, tree frogs stay out of the sun as much as possible.

Are toads frogs?

TOADS AND FROGS ARE CLOSELY RELATED, as you might guess from the way they look. But they are not the same. Toads have dry, warty skin, and frogs have smooth, moist skin. And frogs are much better at jumping and leaping than toads.

This green toad feeds on insects. It catches them by flicking out its sticky tongue and dragging them into its mouth.

Are toads tasty?

Many toads have poison glands in special lumps behind their eyes. If a dog or another animal grabs the toad, it gets a squirt of foul-tasting liquid in its mouth, and drops the toad at once.

Do snakes eat toads?

Snakes don't mind the poison that toads produce. So toads have to find another way of defending themselves. Many puff up their body, and stand on their toes to make themselves look too big to swallow.

Why do toads dig burrows?

Many toads hide from their enemies during the day by digging down into the ground. They burrow into loose soil with their hind feet and snuggle in backwards. The cool, moist soil stops their skin from drying out in hot weather.

This little toad's colouring is a good disguise on the forest floor.

When do toads eat?

Most toads sleep during the day, and hunt at night. They eat all kinds of animals, as long as they can fit them into their mouths. You will often see toads near lamps or other lights. They snap up insects that are attracted by the light.

DID YOU KNOW?
Animals are sometimes given the wrong names by mistake. The horned toad looks rather like a toad, but it is really a lizard. Toads do not have tails.

How big is a cane toad?

A cane toad is about the size of a dinner plate. It is one of the largest toads in the world. The cane toad eats just about anything smaller than itself, including mice, beetles, crickets, and worms.

Do toads jump well?

Toads cannot jump as well as frogs. Many frogs can jump several times the length of their body. But this common toad, like most others, gets about by taking little hops.

Are toads useful?

Most toads stuff as much food into their mouths as they can. For this reason, many farmers and gardeners use them to keep the number of insects down. In Hawaii toads have been used to control the number of beetles damaging the sugar crop.

Where do toads keep their eggs?

Most toads lay their eggs in pools of water, and leave them there. But the female Surinam toad lives under water and keeps her eggs in chambers in the spongy skin on her back until they turn into tiny toads.

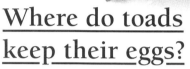

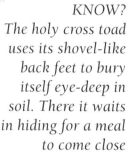

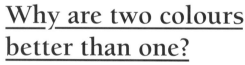

DID YOU KNOW?
The holy cross toad uses its shovel-like back feet to bury itself eye-deep in soil. There it waits in hiding for a meal to come close enough to snatch.

Why are two colours better than one?

The Oriental fire-bellied toad's green back hides it well in the forest. But if an enemy attacks it, it flashes its bright red belly. Most animals know that bright colours mean poison.

TOAD FACTS

- The smallest toad in the world is from Mozambique. It grows no bigger than 24 mm (1 in) long.

- The spadefoot toad gets its name from its feet, which are perfectly shaped for digging.

- Toads and frogs are very noisy. The mating calls of some can be heard more than a kilometre (half a mile) away.

- Some toads can take in water through the skin of their belly just by sitting on damp ground.

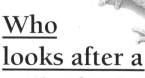

Who looks after a midwife's babies?

The female midwife toad lays her eggs on the male's hind legs. He carries them around while they are developing, then he takes them to a pond where the tadpoles hatch and swim free.

Why do birds sing?

BIRDS SING FOR ALL kinds of reasons, such as attracting a mate, or telling other birds to keep out of their territory. Often, many birds live in the same area. When they all sing in a dawn chorus, the sound can be very loud indeed.

A long beak can reach inside flowers for nectar.

When do birds hum?

Hummingbirds hover by a flower while they feed. They have to beat their wings up to 50 times a second – so fast that you can hardly see them. But you can hear the humming sound the beating wings make.

What does an oxpecker peck?

Oxpeckers eat the ticks and flies that bother many large animals living on the plains of Africa. So the animals let these birds walk all over them, pecking up the pests.

How do pelicans fish?

When a pelican spots a fish below the surface of the water it dives straight towards it. It opens its beak wide and its throat pouch swells to trap the fish like a net.

The water that rushes into a pelican's beak with the fish can weigh more than the bird.

When do male frigatebirds go red?

When they see a female frigatebird. The male has a red pouch at his throat that he can blow up like a balloon. The bigger and redder it is, the more attractive he is to a female.

Do wagtails hunt?

Wagtails live by streams and lakes. They wait on a rock or bank, and dart out over the water to snap up passing insects with their long, pointed beaks.

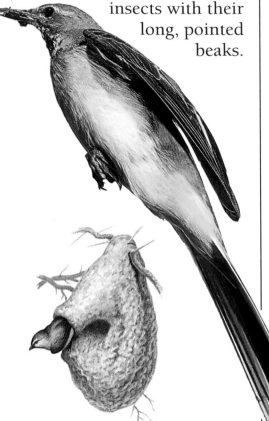

Why should a home have two doors?

Cape penduline tits build a large false entrance so enemies think there is no way in. The real entrance is smaller, and easy to miss.

What makes a bird's hair stand on end?

Many cockatoos make the tuft of feathers at the back of their head stand on end when they become excited or angry. They do this to warn off other birds.

When does a peacock walk backwards?

When he is trying to charm a peahen. He opens his train of dazzling feathers with his back to her, then walks closer and closer. At last he whirls around and displays the train in all its glory.

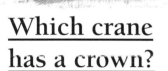

Which crane has a crown?

The black crowned crane's head is topped with straw-coloured feathers that look like a crown. But it is the black feathers at the front that give this bird its name.

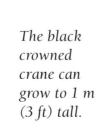

The black crowned crane can grow to 1 m (3 ft) tall.

Doves and pigeons belong to the same family of birds.

How can flamingos eat upside down?

A flamingo's beak works like a sieve. It lowers it into water upside down to trap tiny plants and shrimps. The bird's swallowing muscles are so strong that it can gulp up fish without raising its head.

How does a dove drink?

Doves have pointed beaks for feeding on seeds and leaves. But they can also use them like a straw, to suck up water.

Where do emperors keep their eggs?

Emperor penguins live in Antarctica. The female goes off to feed as soon as she has laid her egg, so the male keeps it warm by carrying it on his feet. After the chick has hatched, it stays warm in the same way.

BIRD FACTS

- The most common bird is the seed-eating quelea of Africa. There are about 10,000 million queleas in total.

- All birds have four toes. But the arrangement of the toes tells us whether the bird is best at perching, climbing, or paddling.

- The kea of southern New Zealand often hangs around ski resorts, where it rolls around and plays in the snow.

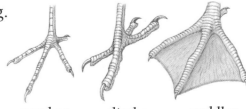

percher   climber   paddler

Are birds dangerous?

BIRDS OF PREY ARE dangerous, but only to small or medium-sized animals. These meat eaters have long claws for stabbing and gripping their prey and sharp, powerful beaks for tearing it apart. Some may fly hundreds of kilometres a day searching for a meal.

The eagle's high nest gives it a good view so it can look out for other birds.

How do owls hunt in the dark?

Owls could probably hunt blindfolded. They hear the slightest rustle of feet and can home in on a target using their hearing alone. But owls have very good eyesight, too, and they can see clearly even on dark nights.

Which bird makes a big splash?

With its wings folded back and its feet forward, an osprey hits the water and vanishes in a fountain of spray. If it has aimed well it will rise into the air with a fish held firmly in its claws.

Whose nest looks like an unmade bed?

An eagle piles big sticks in a heap to make a nest. It looks messy, but it's strong and lasts for several years. Eagles build their nests at the top of dead trees, so the eggs are fairly safe.

DID YOU KNOW? Birds of prey can see about four times as well as people. Some hawks can spot a grasshopper 100 m (330 ft) away.

The Egyptian vulture is one of the few birds known to use tools.

Do birds eat eggs?

Egyptian vultures don't wait for their prey to hatch. These vultures love to eat the eggs of other large birds, such as ostriches. They use rocks as tools, throwing them at the eggs to smash the shells.

Who likes fast food?

Peregrine falcons mostly hunt other birds. They dive at their prey from above, tucking their wings back to gain extra speed. The prey falls to the ground when it is hit, and the falcon follows to snatch up its prize.

What do eagles eat?

Most eagles hunt animals small enough to pick up and carry away. But if they manage to kill a larger animal, they eat it on the spot. Eagles kill with their claws and use their sharp beaks to cut through the flesh.

A secretary bird has longer legs than any other bird of prey.

Do secretaries dance?

When a secretary bird is looking for a mate it does little dances on the ground and makes fabulous swoops and dives in the air.

Which is the heaviest bird of prey?

The Andean condor is the heaviest bird of prey. It weighs up to 12 kg (26 lb). Condors are weak fliers, and rain soon grounds them. They have to spread their wings out to dry before they can take off.

What does a harpy eagle hunt?

The mighty harpy eagle can thread its way among trees at up to 70 km/h (43 mph) chasing a monkey. It also plucks sloths, snakes, and opossums out of the branches.

BIRD OF PREY FACTS

- Vultures hunt during the heat of the day when they can save energy by gliding on warm air currents, called thermals.

- Owls have one eye set higher on their heads than the other. They use the two different images they see to work out how far away an object is.

- Up to 100 vultures at a time may feed on the carcass (dead body) of one animal. If there is more than enough food, these birds sometimes eat so much that they can't fly.

45

What is a snake?

SNAKES ARE REPTILES that have no hands or feet. They move about by wriggling or creeping. A snake is mostly backbone, with a head at one end and a whip-like tail at the other. Many snakes have a poisonous bite.

Can snakes catch birds?

A tree boa can catch birds on the wing. It waits in a tree until a bird flies close by. Then it flings itself straight at its victim, wraps itself around it, and squeezes it to death.

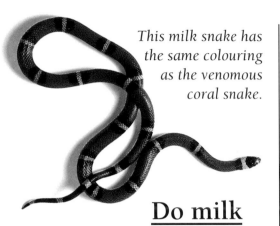

This milk snake has the same colouring as the venomous coral snake.

Why is a vine snake green?

Vine snakes live in trees. Their green skin blends in with the colour of the trees, making them difficult to see.

Do milk snakes drink milk?

They never touch the stuff! They only hang around cowsheds because of the mice that live there. Milk snakes kill their victims by constricting (squeezing) them. Then they swallow them whole.

If a cobra is alarmed it rears up, spreads the hood of skin on the sides of its neck, and hisses.

Do rattlesnakes make friends?

Not really. Rattlesnakes spend most of their time alone. In winter, however, they gather in large groups to sleep through the cold weather. Sometimes as many as 1,000 snakes will hole up together in a single den. This helps them to stay warm.

Why don't desert snakes get burnt?

They would if they crawled through the hot sand. Instead they move by side-winding. They arch their bodies from side to side, so they hardly touch the ground.

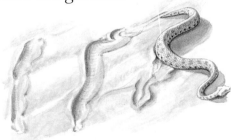

DID YOU KNOW?
It's not the snake charmer's music that makes a cobra dance and sway. The fact is, a cobra is almost deaf. Although it seems to be following the music, all it's really doing is following the pipe as the charmer waves it slowly back and forth.

Baby snakes have a special egg tooth for breaking out of their eggshell.

Is a baby cobra dangerous?

A cobra is deadly from the moment it hatches. Like most snakes, cobras lay eggs and then leave them to hatch. As soon as a baby cobra is out of the egg it has to look after itself. That means attacking and killing other animals to get a meal.

Can snakes fly?

No snakes can fly, but there is one that can glide. It lives in the jungles of Asia and launches itself from the tops of trees. This snake glides through the air on flaps of skin along the sides of its body, and steers by twisting from side to side.

Flying snakes flatten and widen their bodies for gliding.

DID YOU KNOW?
Egg-eating snakes can gulp down eggs twice as big as their head. Their mouth stretches like rubber to take it in. Their jaws are flexible, too – the lower jaw can unhook from the upper one.

SNAKE FACTS

• Snakes stick out their tongues to smell what is in the air.

• Some snakes live in the sea. Their bite can kill a fish in seconds.

• The black mamba is one of the fastest snakes on the ground. It can move at 11km/h (7 mph) – a bit faster than you can walk.

Egg-eating snakes coil their body around an egg to hold it steady.

Can snakes hunt at night?

Many snakes can see better at night than they can in daylight. But some, like this tree boa, have an extra sense. Tiny holes around its lips can feel the body heat of its prey.

How do you milk a snake?

Snakes don't produce milk. But some kinds produce a venom that we use in medicines. People collect the venom by gently squeezing the back of the snake's head.

Do crocodiles cry?

CROCODILES CRY TEARS when they eat, as though they are feeling sorry for their prey. People often use the phrase "crocodile tears" to mean false tears. But the crocodile's tears are just a way of getting rid of the salt from the water that it swallows along with its food!

How do crocs hatch?

Like most reptiles, baby crocodiles have an egg tooth to help them break out of the egg. But if they have difficulty, Mum can help crack the shell.

What do crocs eat?

Baby crocodiles eat insects. As they grow, they catch larger animals, such as frogs and fish. Fully grown crocodiles eat deer, antelopes, and even zebras.

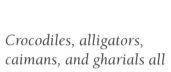

Crocodiles, alligators, caimans, and gharials all belong to the same family.

DID YOU KNOW?
In ancient Egypt, people showed their respect for the Nile crocodile by giving their god Sebek a crocodile head in all the pictures and statues that they made of him.

Do crocodiles clean their teeth?

They don't have to – a plover like this one will do it for them. The crocodile lets the bird pick its teeth for scraps of food. Having its teeth cleaned may be good for the crocodile too.

What is a gharial?

The gharial is a cousin of the crocodile. It lives in rivers in northern India. A gharial has a long, slender snout full of dagger-like teeth, which it uses to catch fish.

Crocodiles yawn when they're hot, not when they're tired.

Do crocodiles yawn?

Crocodiles don't yawn because they are tired. But when they bask in the sun they get hot. So they open their jaws wide to help them cool down. A crocodile can lose heat quickly from the inside of its mouth.

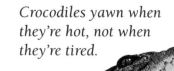

How do caimans hide?

This caiman, like all crocodiles and alligators, has its eyes and nose on the top of its head, so it can see and breathe when most of its body is under water. It glides slowly and quietly up to its prey, then suddenly attacks.

Can crocodiles jump?

Only in water. They use their strong, flat tails to push themselves up out of the water so they can grab animals from overhanging branches. They can swim fast, too. But on land crocodiles are clumsy animals.

An alligator's eyes are on the top of its head.

Can crocodiles chew?

Crocodile teeth are perfect for grabbing and holding prey, but not for chewing. A crocodile usually drags prey into the water and holds it under until it drowns. Then it tears off chunks of flesh and swallows them whole.

Why do crocodiles swallow stones?

Scientists have found stones in the stomachs of crocodiles and alligators. They think these animals may swallow the stones to help them grind up food.

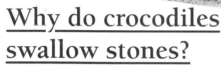

Do crocs make nests?

Many crocodiles make nests for their eggs. The mother guards the eggs, but when they hatch she carries her babies gently to the water, then leaves them to take care of themselves.

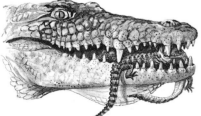

CROCODILE FACTS

- Crocodiles often lose teeth, but new ones grow quickly. A crocodile can have more than fifty complete sets of teeth in a lifetime.

- Estuarine crocodiles are the biggest of all. They can grow up to 8 m (27 ft) long.

- When an alligator dives, it clamps its nostrils shut, and closes its ear tubes. A flap at the back of its throat stops water getting into its lungs.

Do dragons exist?

NO ONE HAS EVER FOUND PROOF of flying, fire-breathing dragons like those of legends. But take a look at a lizard and you will understand where people got the idea.

A gecko can't blink, so it wipes its eyes with its tongue instead.

When do lizards lose their tails?

When they are in serious danger, many lizards have a great trick. If an enemy catches a lizard by the tail, it breaks off. The tail keeps wriggling while the lizard runs off to live another day.

Do geckos bark?

Geckos are little lizards that can click, chirp, and bark. They use these noises when courting a mate or defending their home. Very few reptiles can make this many different sounds.

How do chameleons change colour?

A chameleon's skin has cells containing colour pigments. When the cells get bigger or smaller, the skin colour changes. But nobody knows exactly what controls the cells.

Are frills useful?

They are to a frilled lizard. If it can, it runs away from danger. But if it is cornered, the lizard hisses and raises its frill like a huge collar. This scares off most enemies, even though the lizard is really harmless.

DID YOU KNOW?
Some lizards, such as this glass lizard, have no legs at all. They slink about like snakes, or burrow like worms.

Wing-like flaps of skin help the lizard escape in an emergency.

Can lizards fly?

Flying lizards can't really fly because they don't have wings. But they can make long, controlled downward glides using flaps of skin along the sides of their bodies.

Why do lizards stick their tongues out?

Lizards stick their tongues out to taste the air. But this blue-tongued lizard can also scare off its enemies with its blue tongue.

The basilisk uses its tail to help it balance.

Can lizards walk on water?

A basilisk can walk – or rather run – on water. It skitters over the surface on its huge back feet at up to 12 km/h (7.5 mph).

Which lizard cries tears of blood?

The horned toad is really a lizard. When an enemy, such as a bird, attacks this lizard it sometimes squirts blood from its eyes. It sounds odd, but attackers are often so surprised that they simply give up.

How long is a lizard's tongue?

A chameleon's tongue is longer than its body. It can shoot out and back to catch an insect in 4/100 of a second. That's faster than you can blink.

The pricklenape agama's toes have spiky scales to help it grip branches.

How do lizards climb?

Lizards that live in trees have long toes, with sharp claws for gripping. Some also use their tail to grip with, coiling it around branches like an extra arm.

LIZARD FACTS

- The collared lizard of North America escapes from danger by getting up on its hind legs and running off at high speed.

- The largest lizard is the Komodo dragon from Indonesia. It grows up to 3 m (10 ft) long, and can kill wild pigs and deer with its fangs and sharp claws.

- The shingleback lizard has a short, triangular tail that looks like a head. It's difficult at first to tell which end is which.

Who lives in a box?

TORTOISES AND TURTLES live in a box of thick shell, which covers their body like a suit of armour. Only the head, legs, and tail stick out. If danger threatens, tortoises and turtles can pull these inside, too.

What is a terrapin?

A terrapin is a freshwater turtle. It eats plants, worms, carrion (dead animals), and anything else it can find. People often keep terrapins as pets, but most soon die of malnutrition (an unbalanced diet).

Do turtles smell bad?

There is a small turtle in North America that can make a very unpleasant smell. It's called a stinkpot turtle. When a bird or other animal picks it up, it releases the scent. Usually the enemy drops the turtle at once.

DID YOU KNOW?
Depending on where they live, turtles and tortoises have differently shaped feet.

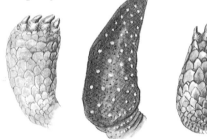

Land   Sea   Fresh water

DID YOU KNOW?
Leatherback turtles spend most of their lives at sea. They only come ashore to lay their eggs.

Why do turtles snap?

Snapping turtles lurk at the bottom of rivers or ponds, snapping up fish as they swim by. Some snapping turtles even attack human hands or feet.

How do turtles fish?

Alligator snappers sit on the bottom of swamps and creeks with their mouths wide open. When a curious fish comes along to look at a bright pink, wriggling worm, the turtle grabs it in its powerful jaws. The worm is really a part of the snapper's tongue.

This little fish is about to have a nasty surprise.

Why do turtles cry?

Marine (sea-living) turtles swallow salt water as they feed. Too much salt is bad for them, so, like crocodiles, they cry salty tears to get rid of it.

What shape is a tortoise's shell?

Giant tortoises on islands where food plants grow on the ground have a gently curved shell. Those on islands where food grows higher up have a groove at the front of the shell, so they can raise their heads.

What if a shell is too small for you?

A turtle with a small shell has a real problem. The big-headed turtle's head is far too big for its shell. Luckily, the head is covered in extra tough skin.

Hinge

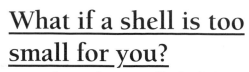

Can shells bend?

The hinge-back tortoise can swing part of its shell down at the back to protect the rear of its body. Then it nudges the front of its shell against a rock to guard its head.

Giant tortoises have been known to live for more than a century.

Big-headed turtles look as though they are in the wrong shell!

DID YOU KNOW?
A fully grown giant tortoise can be a metre long and weigh nearly as much as three people. But a fully grown leatherback turtle is as heavy as a small car and its flippers span about 3.5 m (12 ft).

Can a shell be a door?

Gopher tortoises share their homes with frogs and mice, but they can keep out snakes by using their shell as a door.

TURTLE FACTS

- Many river turtles soak up oxygen through their skin. They can stay under water for days without coming up for air.

- Green turtles feed along the coast of South America, but they travel 2,200 km (1,367 miles) across the Atlantic to lay their eggs on Ascension Island.

- Turtles spend hours basking in the sun to warm their bodies up for hunting.

Do fish breathe air?

FISH CAN'T BREATHE AIR, because they don't have lungs. Instead they have gills, which they use to take oxygen from the water. You can tell their gills are working by watching the flaps behind their head open and close as water flows past.

How does a filefish hide?

The filefish has a clever trick for avoiding enemies. It hides in the seaweed and sways gently in the current, just like a piece of weed. From the front, the fish is so thin it is almost invisible.

This ribbon eel can coil backwards into very small spaces.

How do eels get meals?

They smell them. Eels have a better sense of smell than any other fish. By day they hide in caves, or nooks and crannies along rocky coasts. At night they come out to hunt for food.

When the porcupine fish is full of air or water, its sharp spines stick out.

The ribbon eel is a kind of moray eel. Moray eels often hide in crevices with only their heads sticking out, waiting for prey to swim past.

Which fish blows itself up?

When a porcupine fish is in danger it puffs itself up by swallowing water, or even air. This makes it far too big for other fish to swallow.

Which eels live in gardens?

Garden eels live in groups, with their tails buried in the sand and their heads pointed into the current. A crowd of them looks like a patch of tall grass.

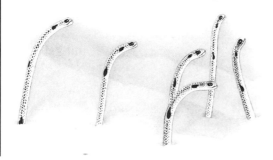

Do fish lay eggs?

Some fish lay hundreds of eggs, which drift about in the sea and are gobbled up by all kinds of hungry animals. Other fish lay fewer eggs, and keep them in a nest where they can watch over them. These eggs have a better chance of hatching without being eaten.

Can dads give birth?

Male sea horses have a pouch on their belly, in which the female lays her eggs. Then she swims off, leaving Dad to look after them. When the young hatch, they pop out of their father's pouch.

How can a stone kill?

Stonefish look just like stones on the sea bed. But if you stepped on one, the poison in the spines on its fins could kill you in less than two hours.

Do fish sleep?

Fish sleep with their eyes open because they have no eyelids. But they can shut their pupils. This dogfish has narrowed its pupil to let in less light while it snoozes.

Would you eat a deadly dish?

Japanese people try to cut out the poisonous parts of *fugu*, or death pufferfish, before they eat it. But *fugu* still causes about twenty deaths every year.

Can fish fish?

Anglerfish can. They sit on reefs with their tongues out, looking like juicy, wriggling worms. If a curious fish swims close the anglerfish opens its huge mouth and sucks it in.

This viperfish attracts prey in the darkness of the deep sea by producing its own light.

Which fish has extra teeth?

The deep-sea viperfish attacks fish bigger than itself. Its jaws can swing wide open like a door. Inside the mouth, long teeth curve backwards to stop prey escaping, and extra teeth in the throat grip the meal and help push it down towards the fish's huge stomach.

FISH FACTS

- A fully grown electric eel can give off a shock powerful enough to light up a whole house.

- Most fish are protected by a layer of hard, thin scales. A few, such as catfish, have no scales at all.

- Some fish are so well adapted to living at the bottom of the sea that if they come to the surface too quickly, they pop!

What do sharks eat?

YOU MAY HAVE HEARD STORIES of sharks eating people, but most sharks eat much smaller prey, which is easier to catch. Some sharks feed on plankton (microscopic plants and animals) and some eat fish, including other sharks, and their cousins, the rays. It is very rare for sharks to eat people.

Most sharks have a streamlined shape, like this spinner shark.

What's great, white, and deadly?

The great white shark has a reputation for killing people. Its jaws are 300 times as powerful as yours, and its razor-sharp teeth are as long as your fingers. This fearsome shark feeds mostly on fish, seals, and other sharks, and seldom attacks people.

How do sharks trick fish?

The spinner shark has a neat trick to fool its prey. It charges into a school of fish, then suddenly begins to spin around. Fish trying to escape have no idea which way the shark is headed next.

What are rays?

Rays are closely related to sharks, and like them, they have skeletons made of bendy cartilage instead of hard bones. Rays have flat bodies, well suited to feeding on the bottom of the sea.

Which shark lashes its prey with its tail?

A thresher shark's tail is as long as its body. It threshes (lashes) it around in the water to herd fish into a tight group. Then the shark slices through the group, gulping as many as it can.

Which shark looks like seaweed?

The Australian wobbegong lies on the sea bed waiting to grab its prey. It has so many bristles on its head that fish and crabs often mistake it for seaweed, and swim right up to its jaws.

Can rays fly?

As they flap their huge wings slowly up and down, manta rays often seem to be flying under water. They sometimes leap right out of the water, but fall back with a great splash!

How do sharks find lunch?

Most sharks have an amazing sense of smell. They could smell a single drop of blood, even if it were mixed in a bathtub full of water. They also have pits next to their eyes, which can feel the ripples of electricity that other fish make as they swim.

You can see why the hammerhead shark got its name.

What does a hammerhead eat?

Hammerhead sharks eat fish, such as catfish and rays. Many rays have poisonous spines on their tails that protect them from most predators. But the spines don't seem to bother hammerhead sharks.

Epaulette sharks grow to about 1 m (3 ft) long.

Can sharks walk?

The epaulette shark, like many small sharks, feeds on the sea bed. It uses its side fins rather like legs to walk along as it searches for sea urchins, crabs, small fish, and other food.

Do sharks like blood?

Sharks don't mind blood at all. In fact a bleeding fish, or other animal, draws them like a magnet. As they rush to feed, they often get so excited that they bite anything that moves, including each other.

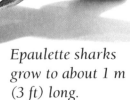

DID YOU KNOW?
Sharks live mostly at sea, but some kinds swim up rivers from time to time. Bull sharks have been found hundreds of kilometres up the Amazon river in South America.

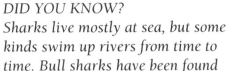

This eagle ray looks as graceful as a bird as it swims through the water on its broad, flat wings.

Are rays dangerous?

Most rays are harmless to humans. But stingrays have poisonous spines on their tails to defend themselves against anything that comes too close. The spines are connected to poison sacs, and they are very painful if they touch you as you swim past.

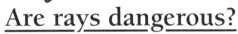

SHARK & RAY FACTS

- Sharks are constantly losing teeth and growing new ones. They may get through more than 20,000 teeth during a lifetime.

- The Atlantic torpedo ray can stun its prey with more than 200 volts of electricity. 200 volts could almost run a television set!

- The largest shark is the whale shark, which can grow up to 18 m (60 ft) long.

Where do crabs live?

CRABS, LOBSTERS, PRAWNS, woodlice, and barnacles all belong to the group of animals called crustaceans. Most crustaceans live in the sea, but some prefer fresh water, and a few have even adapted to life on land.

Male lobsters have much bigger claws than female lobsters.

This arrowhead crab's legs can reach out much further sideways than they can reach forwards.

Do crabs always walk sideways?

Many crabs can go forwards, backwards, and sideways. But their legs are close together, and they can only take small steps forwards or backwards. Most crabs can take bigger steps sideways, and so run faster.

Which spider has two extra legs?

Spiders have eight legs. But spider crabs, like all crabs, have ten. Two legs have pincers on the ends, which the crab uses to grab and hold food. The rest are for walking and running.

Where do lobsters hide?

Lobsters spend most of their time in rocky nooks and crannies. Their favourite hideout is a sandy hole under a rock. Once they have dug a hole just the right shape, lobsters only come out to find food.

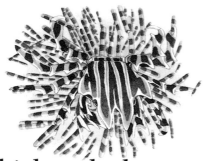

Which crabs have urchin friends?

The Adam's urchin crab clings to a sea urchin for safety. The striped patterns on the crab's back and legs blend in well with the urchin's spines, and most predators avoid sea urchins because of their sting. This means the crab is safe too.

Spiny spider crabs are among the largest crabs.

Which shrimp is a giant?

The mantis shrimp is at least three times the size of most other shrimps. It lives in shallow water, not far from sandy shores, and crushes its prey with its spiny front claws.

This decorator crab covers itself with pieces of plant and sponge from the sea bed. Tiny bristles hold all the pieces in place.

Why are crabs like medieval knights?

Crabs, like medieval knights, wear armour that's tough enough to protect them. And a crab's shell is jointed, just like armour. But unlike knights, crabs can only take their armour off when they moult.

What do crabs eat?

Crabs aren't the slightest bit fussy about what they eat. They nibble all the leftovers they can find on the bottom of the sea. They also catch fish and worms, and crunch up all kinds of other little animals with their pincers.

Is a crayfish a fish?

Many animals with the word fish in their name are not fish at all, including shellfish, crayfish, and cuttlefish. Crayfish are freshwater relatives of lobsters. They live under stones or in burrows in streams and ponds.

When do lobsters travel in trains?

When spiny lobsters like these migrate to deeper water to lay their eggs, they travel in long trains, often hanging on to the one in front. They sometimes travel more than 150 km (90 miles) in this way.

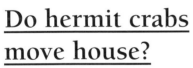

Crayfish look very much like their cousins, the lobsters.

Do hermit crabs move house?

Hermit crabs don't have their own shells, so they look for empty snail or whelk shells to live in. You can't often tempt a hermit crab out of its home, but when it finds a better shell, it scuttles rapidly out of its old home and into the new one.

CRAB FACTS

- The pea crab has a smooth, round body no bigger than a pea. It lives inside the shells of mussels and clams.

- The robber crab spends most of its time on land. It is said to feed on young coconuts, climbing up palm trees and snipping the stalks of the coconuts with its claws.

- The giant Japanese spider crab is the biggest crab in the world. It can grow to up to 3 m (10 ft) from leg tip to leg tip. That's further than you can jump.

INDEX

GLOSSARY

amphibians *animals that live on land and in water, such as frogs and toads*

arachnids *animals with simple eyes and eight legs, such as spiders, scorpions, and ticks*

blubber *the layer of fat just under the skin of a mammal, such as a walrus, that keeps it warm*

camouflage *colours and patterns which match an animal's background and help disguise it*

carcass *the dead body of a animal*

carrion *meat which has not been freshly killed*

cold-blooded animals *animals that need the sun to warm their bodies*

constricting *squeezing to death, a method some snakes use to kill their prey*

fertile *able to produce young*

gills *the organs that some animals, such as fish, use for taking in oxygen from water*

hibernation *a sleep that lasts through winter*

larvae *the grub-like young of some animals, which will develop into very different adults*

loping *slow running, with a long stride, as wolves do, to cover long distances*

malnutrition *lack of nourishment, caused by an unbalanced diet*

mammals *animals with warm blood, such as elephants, humans, and whales*

mantle *the part of a mollusc that makes the shell*

marine *sea-living plants or animals*

mollusc *a soft-bodied animal, such as a snail, that often has a shell*

operculum *a protective cover, such as the disc on a snail's foot that blocks the entrance to its shell*

parasite *an animal or plant that lives on another*

plankton *tiny, floating sea animals and plants*

prey *an animal hunted for food*

prehensile tails *tails that can grasp*

primates *advanced mammals, such as apes, monkeys, and humans*

reptiles *cold-blooded animals, such as tortoises, snakes, lizards, and crocodiles*

siphon *the tube that an octopus has for breathing, feeding, and moving*

thermals *warm currents in the air which some birds, such as vultures, use to help them glide*

underfur *the thick fur that some animals have next to their skin to keep them warm*

warm-blooded animals *animals whose body temperature is always the same*

ACKNOWLEDGEMENTS

Dorling Kindersley would like to thank
the following for their photographs:

Jane Burton, Geoff Dann, Mike Dunning, Frank Greenaway,
Colin Keates, Dave King, Karl Shone, Kim Taylor, Jerry Young

and the following for their illustrations:

Julie Anderson, John Bendall-Brunello, Ruth Benton,
John Davis, Angelika Elsbach, Gill Elsbury, Jane Gedye,
John Hutchinson, Mark Iley, Ruth Lindsay, Polly Noakes,
Valerie Price, Colin Woolf, Dan Wright.